My Family is Changing
Coping With Divorce

SUPPORT RESPECT

written by Craig Ashley Hill
and Louise Joy Hill
illustrated by Jennifer Taylor

Acknowledgements

Contributors:
Dr. Gina Sartore, Ph.D.
Dr. Sue Connor, B.A. (Hons), M.Clin.Psych, M.A.Ps.S
Vickie A Moore
Cameron Hill
Kirrily Taylor
Ross Scott

Edited By:
Marielle D. Marne / A-1 Editing

Illustrations and Book Design By:
Jennifer Taylor
www.nwglobal.com/jenart/

Contents

A Message from Us

Louise and I have been married for eight years and have been blessed with three children: Cameron, an eight year old boy (he constantly reminds everyone that he is eight and a half) and twin girls, Kayla and Talia aged two.

I was previously married and have three children from that marriage: Peter, aged 17, Jessica, aged 16 and Steven, aged 15.

Louise and I are both firm believers that keeping communication flowing (or open) with your children throughout a separation or divorce is paramount for a "healthy divorce." We consider a healthy divorce to be one that allows all parties (especially the children, if there are any) to move on with a positive outlook on the future.

We believe that when it comes to a divorce, children should be told the truth. Sure, you may not want to give the nitty gritty details of who did what to whom, however, the whispers in the kitchen will be picked up on by the children, and you may force your children to withdraw at a time when you need to know exactly what is on their minds. Our advice is to treat your children like people, not children. Keep them informed, support them and allow them to support you. This does NOT mean that you should lay all your troubles on their shoulders or allow them to enter into arguments or force them to take sides; common sense should prevail!

This is the first book we have written, and the first in the "My Family is Changing" series. The series is dedicated to equipping children and young adolescents with information that will enhance their life skills.

Craig and Louise Hill

Foreword

Maybe you are reading this because a friend or an adult you know gave it to you.

Or maybe you found it for yourself. Either way, if you are reading this book, it is probably because there are changes going on in your family right now.

Change can be really scary, especially if it is related to something very important like your family. Perhaps things are happening that you don't quite understand, or that make you feel bad, and perhaps you don't exactly know what is going to happen next.

When things scare us, it's good to talk them over with people who will listen to us and try to understand our fears. But that can be difficult if the people we usually talk to are part of what's making us scared. Also, if people in your family are having problems, maybe you don't want to talk to just one parent at a time—maybe you want to get everyone together to talk things over. That can be really hard, too.

We hope that this book will give you some more information about what is going on and make things less scary. We also hope that you can use the ideas in this book to talk to someone who can make you feel better: parents, grandparents, brothers and sisters, or just a good friend.

Some other places you can get help: your school or church; a friend's parent if you know them really well; or you could call
Kid's Help Phone 1 800 668 6868 (U.S.A) or
the Kid's Helpline on 1 800 551 800 (Australia)
or look them up on the internet.

Gina Sartore, PhD.

What is a family?

Who are the people in your family? One dictionary defines a family as a group of individuals living under one roof. There are other definitions, however, and we would like to think that a family (when living under one roof) is comprised of individuals united by love.

There are many forms in which such a family may take. Traditionally, it may be a father, mother and children; but family units may consist of grandparents, parents and children; parents of the same sex and children; uncles, aunts and children and others. The main point of which to take note is that the family, no matter how it is comprised, is held together by individuals who love and support each other.

Things Start to Change

When living as a member of a family, it is easy to become concerned that the situation may change from the way it is now. Just as you will sometimes fight with your brothers and sisters or friends at school, so too will your parents become unhappy with each other. And though your parents are arguing or fighting, this does not mean that they are headed for divorce. It may simply mean that they are experiencing additional stress.

Remember, your parents have pressures that you may not even have realized existed, such as paying bills and going to work. It puts that fight that you had with your sister over borrowing her jeans into perspective, doesn't it?

The main point here is that you should not confuse your parent's arguments for the possibility of them divorcing. Your parents will let you know when their relationship has changed to that extent.

As much as we want our lives to stay as they are in a happy family, sometimes this is just not possible. Although we want things to stay as they are, it may not be fair to ask your parents to stay together when they may no longer be in love with each other or wish to stay together. Some people believe that it is much better for parents to live separately rather than stay together when neither wishes to remain in the relationship.

Your Parents Decide to Live Separately

Your parents may decide to take a break from their relationship with each other and live separately. This can occur on a trial basis (trial separation), or they may decide to make this separation permanent.

Some couples decide that when they have been apart for some time, they really want and need to remain together after all.

You may ask yourself, "Why do my parents want to live apart, don't they love each other anymore, or don't they love me anymore?"

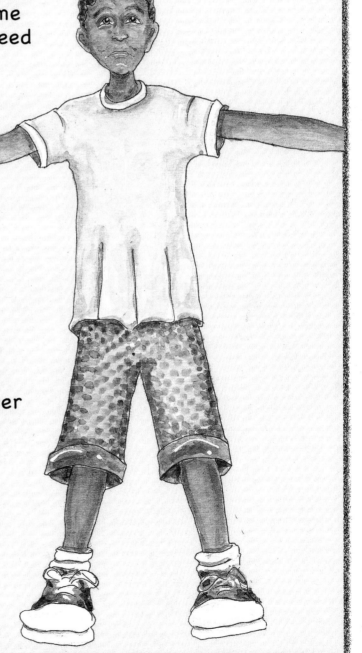

What you must realize is that your parents are people too, and they need to love and feel love from the partner they are with. Sometimes they find that they don't love each other anymore; sometimes they find that they can't be together without arguing or fighting.

Whatever the reason, your parents may decide that living separately for the time being could be best for the entire family.

Just because your parents decide to live separately to start with does not mean that it will always be the case, and the reason that they decide to live separately is never because they don't love you anymore.

Your Parents Decide To Separate Permanently

After your parents have lived separately for some time, they may decide to make that separation permanent. Your parents may decide to live apart for years without ever getting divorced, however, when your parents decide that they will never be getting back together it is usual for a divorce to occur.

Remember, though it may seem like it at first, getting divorced does not mean that the world is going to end. It means that your parents have realized that they no longer wish to live together as a couple, and they wish to open a new chapter in their lives where they live apart from each other and wish to allow each other the opportunity to find someone else to share their lives with.

It does not mean, however, that they don't wish to share their lives with you. Of course, your family unit is likely not going to be the same again, but just as your parents would wish you to be happy in your life, you should wish for your parents to be happy. It may be that your parents would be happiest separated or even divorced.

IT IS NOT YOUR FAULT!

When your parents break up, it is typical for people to ask why it has happened or what they could have done to make things different. There may be many reasons why your parents have decided to break up.

Your parents may be arguing or fighting a lot of the time and now decide that they are a lot happier living apart from each other. Your parents may no longer be in love with each other, they may say that they have no reason at all and say "there is no reason for it; it just happened" or say "...... we grew apart". Whatever the reason, it is very important for you to realize that it WAS NOT your fault!

You may think that if you were better behaved, did what you were told or didn't fight with your brothers and sisters so much, then your parents would still want to be together. None of this is true!

No matter what you have done in the past or what you will do in the future, nothing you do will change whether your parents remain together. The choice to live apart was your parent's. It does not change in any way how they feel about you. Of course, your parents will always love you; that will never change.

Remember that above anything else, and it can't be said enough, your parents love you and always will. Your parent's break up is NOT YOUR FAULT!

Your Parent Seems To Be Sad or Angry

When your family changes, it is often difficult to look beyond how you feel. Since you do not know what is going to happen in the future, you may become worried, scared or even angry about the situation your family is in. These are normal feelings, and you should not feel embarrassed or ashamed that you are feeling these emotions.

Your parents may also be experiencing many of these feelings. You may see a parent crying or even hear words said in anger.

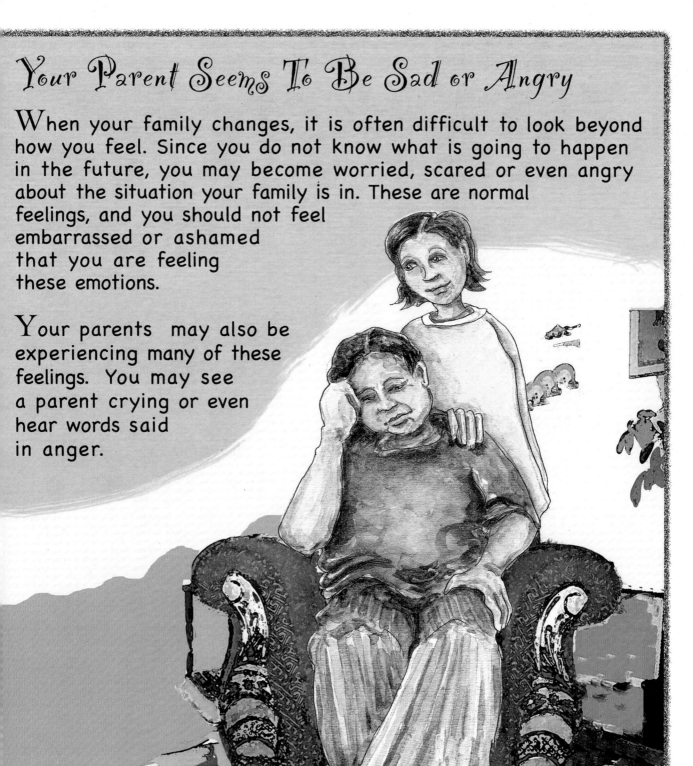

You must remember when this occurs, that they are not angry at you and nothing that your parent is feeling is your fault.

Just as you may feel like being alone when you are sad or angry, so too will your parents. You need to give them the time and space to work things out.

You are not betraying either parent if you give support to one or both of them; this may be as simple as giving them a hug or saying that you understand how they are feeling.

Who Will You Live With?

Just because your parents have decided to live apart does not mean that you will never see one of them again. It will mean however, that decisions will have to made involving where you will live and how you will spend time with each parent. You may hear the word custody a lot. I think it is easiest to describe what custody is by explaining that custody means who will be responsible for your care day to day.

You may be given the opportunity to say with whom you would like to live. If you are given this opportunity, it is important to answer honestly, without worrying about hurting your parent's feelings. Remember, your parents are adults, and they realize that just because you may decide to live with the other parent, they will still usually get to see you very often. It is also important to remember that your parents want you to be happy and want what you want.

Your parents may be given joint custody of you which will allow your parents to spend equal amounts of time with you. For example, you may spend Monday, Tuesday, Wednesday and Thursday with one parent and Friday, Saturday and Sunday with the other parent.

One parent may be given primary care of you and the other parent may be allowed to visit with you on weekends and holidays.

Whatever the care arrangement, it is certain that both parents want you and want you to be happy. So don't be scared of hurting their feelings and tell them how you honestly feel.

If your parents can't decide by themselves how your custody will be arranged, they may ask someone who is specially trained to decide for them (this could occur in a family court or by a court appointed counsellor). This person, along with everyone else involved, cares about you and wants to work out what will be best for you.

Remember that when answering questions about how you feel and what you want nothing that you say is wrong, and nothing that you say will get you or your parents in trouble.

Your Parent(s) Start To See Another Person(s)

We know it may be difficult to understand why your parents have separated. It may be even more difficult to see that one or both of your parents are moving on with their lives. We are sure that some children would prefer that if their parents can't be together, then they should remain alone for the rest of their lives. We think this may have to do with the children holding out hope that their parents may get back together.

There may come a time when your parents start to spend time with, and bring home, a "special friend." It is on these occasions that your parent looks to see what you think of his or her friend, if you have things in common and if you can also become friends.

You should not see this new special friend as a replacement for the other parent, your mother or father is not asking you to do this. You are merely being asked to accept your parent's need for companionship.

Consider this as a chance to see your parent happy and the possibility that this "special friend" may become another adult who you can turn to for friendship, support, advice and maybe even love.

Where Do I Fit Into My Parent(s) Lives?

It is normal for you to be concerned about where you fit into your parent's lives. You fit where you always have – right at the top.

You need to realize that you are the most important thing in your mother and father's lives and that will not change, no matter whether your parents meet "special friends," remarry or even have other children.

If you are concerned about where or how you fit in your parent's lives under these new arrangements, it is best to ask your parents. You should mention any fears you have now or about what is going to occur in the future.

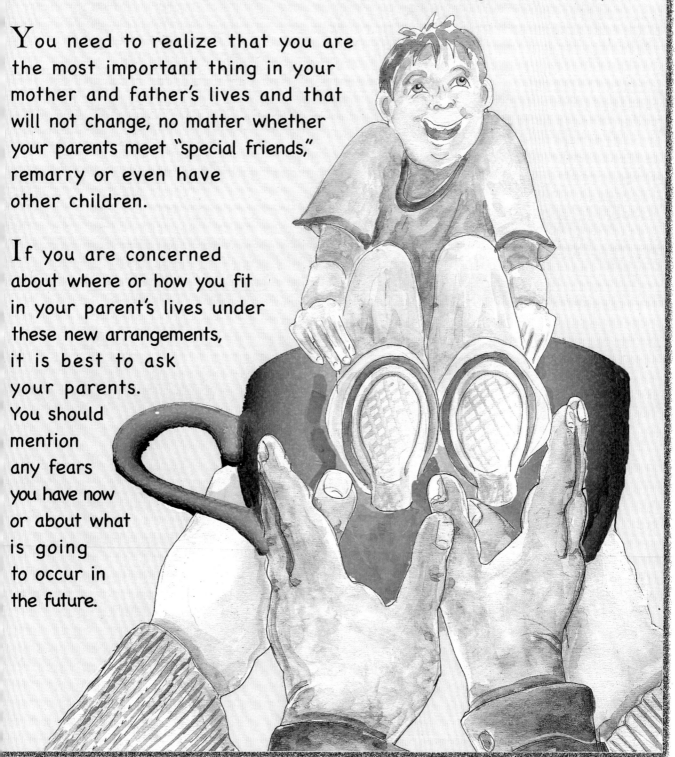

Who Can I Talk To About My Concerns?

If you have any concerns or want your fears about what is going to happen in the future put to rest, you could speak to your parents.

You may not feel comfortable talking with your parents about your fears or concerns and need to talk your feelings over with someone else. You may have a strong relationship with your grandparents, a teacher, a minister, a coach or school counsellor.

You may decide that you need to get some concerns off your chest and talk with your brother or sister, an aunt or uncle or a special, trusted friend. It really does not matter who you speak to, it is important however, not to keep your feelings bottled up inside as this is not healthy for you.

If you decide that you want your information to remain confidential but want the correct advice as to what may occur in the future, but don't want to talk your concerns over with your parents, then your school counsellor is probably a good place to start.

If the school counsellor is not able to answer your question or provide the kind of expertise that you need, then he or she will have the ability to get you into contact with someone who is.

Once your parents have separated or become divorced, you may choose to ask that they honor some promises to you. Some of the things that you may ask for your parents to promise are listed on the following page. An example of how your parent or parents can write these promises to you is also shown at Appendix A and Appendix B.

A Written Promise From Your Parent(s) To You

Once your parents have separated or become divorced, you may choose to ask that they honor some promises to you. An example of how your parent or parents can write these promises to you is also shown at Appendix A.

A promise to :
- Always love you;
- Remind you that it was not your fault that they separated;
- Not make it difficult for you to choose with whom to live;
- Listen to you;
- Try and understand your feelings;
- Treat you like a person (as opposed to a child);
- Take care of you;
- Remind you that you are the most important thing in their lives;
- Not fight with your other parent in front of you;
- Not be mean to your other parent for the sake of being mean;
- Keep appointments for visits;
- Want to see you;
- Try not to embarrass you;
- Be a responsible parent;
- Be a good role-model;
- Let you see your grandparents;
- Not be rude to your other parent's special friend;
- Not criticize your other parent in front of you.

Having a promise written by one or both parents will reassure you of their love for you and their intent to always be there for you. A blank copy of such a promise is at Appendix B. These blank promises may be copied for your parents to use. Even if your parents are not willing to write a promise, it is a good idea to ask them to arrange a separation sponsor or sponsors. These people will be available when you need them. This could be useful as you may feel more at ease talking with someone who knows you personally.

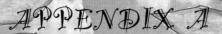

APPENDIX A

A PROMISE WRITTEN TO JOHN AND JOHANNE SMITH

This promise is written to John and Johanne Smith by their parents, Tom and Fiona, upon their separation.

1. We promise to always love you and remind you that our separation was not your fault.
2. We will listen to you and value your opinions. We will try to make it easier for you to choose whom to live with.
3. We will try to understand your feelings and treat you like people (as opposed to children).
4. We will always take care of you and remind you that you are the most important people in our lives.
5. We will try not to fight with each other in front of you, or be purposefully hurtful to each other.
6. We will remain responsible parents and strive to be good role-models for you.
7. We will keep our appointments to see you when scheduled for visits. We want to see you.
8. We will try not to embarrass you.
9. We will not criticize each other in front of you.
10. We will let you see your grandparents, and will schedule visits to ensure this occurs.
11. We will try not to make it difficult for each other's "special friends" or new partners.

We understand that this is also a very difficult time for you. It is not easy to see your parents separate, and for this, we apologize. We will try to make your lives as normal as possible.

We have arranged some separation sponsors (people who you can talk to if you don't feel comfortable talking to either of us). They are:
Aunt Sarah (02) 541298; Mr. Jones (School Counsellor) (02) 543217; and Father O'Leary (02) 543333.

_____   _____
(Signed Tom Smith)   (Signed Fiona Smith)

A promise written to _____ and _____.

This promise is written to _____ and _____ by their parents, _____ and _____ upon their separation.

1. _____
2. _____
3. _____
4. _____
5. _____
6. _____
7. _____
8. _____
9. _____
10. _____
11. _____

We understand that this is also a very difficult time for you. It is not easy to see your parents separate, and for this, we apologize. We will try to make your lives as normal as possible.

We have arranged some separation sponsors (people who you can talk to if you don't feel comfortable talking to either of us). These sponsors are available to talk about issues you are facing or any concerns that you may have.
They are: _____
_____

_____   _____
     (Signed)   (Signed)

Note for Librarians: A cataloguing record for this book is available from
Library and Archives Canada at www.collectionscanada.ca/amicus/index-e.html
ISBN 1-4251-1873-9

Printed in Victoria, BC, Canada. Printed on paper with minimum 30% recycled fibre.
Trafford's print shop runs on "green energy" from solar, wind and other environmentally-friendly power sources.

TRAFFORD
PUBLISHING™

Offices in Canada, USA, Ireland and UK

Book sales for North America and international:
Trafford Publishing, 6E–2333 Government St.,
Victoria, BC V8T 4P4 CANADA
phone 250 383 6864 (toll-free 1 888 232 4444)
fax 250 383 6804; email to orders@trafford.com
Book sales in Europe:
Trafford Publishing (UK) Limited, 9 Park End Street, 2nd Floor
Oxford, UK OX1 1HH UNITED KINGDOM
phone +44 (0)1865 722 113 (local rate 0845 230 9601)
facsimile +44 (0)1865 722 868; info.uk@trafford.com
Order online at:
trafford.com/07-0281

10 9 8 7 6 5 4 3 2